The Job I Need, Needs Me

The Job I Need, Needs Me

Andy Thomas
and Denise K. James

andythomasproductions.com

The Job I Need, Needs Me

Copyright © 2011 by Andy Thomas and Denise K. James

Edited by Sharon Eliza Nichols

Cover design and book layout by Nicole Kansas

All rights reserved.

Published in the United States by Andy Thomas Productions, LLC

ISBN-13: 978-1461133513
ISBN-10: 1461133513

Dedication

*To all who realize that change is inevitable—
that we can always reinvent ourselves with the gifts
and talents we have been given.
Never give up on you.*

Acknowledgements

I'd like to thank Rev. Paul Peck who taught me a prayer phrase in my 20s that has become the cornerstone of my current work. Yes, Paul I learned much from you!

I also wish to thank John Jeppi of The Broadcasting Institute of Maryland for teaching me "if it is to be, it's up to me." A huge thank you to Ingrid, for giving me the foundation, support, and love from which to create the reinvented "me."

I'd also like to directly thank my writer, Denise K. James, who ended up spending months of breakfasts getting my ideas and words into print.

To my parents: Thank you for not panicking too much when I said I wanted to go to broadcasting school to begin a radio career, way back in 1979.

I'd also like to thank all of you who have walked this path of discovery with me, including my thousands of radio and television viewers and listeners and my staff of creatively amazing individuals.

Finally, thank you to God for always pushing me to use these talents, and for sending along the little lessons that taught me the value of passion, for life and career.

Andy Thomas

I'd like to thank my mom and the rest of my family for encouraging me to be a writer and introducing me to the power of words. I'd like to thank Andy for believing that I could co-write this book even when I felt overwhelmed! I'd like to thank my friends simply for being fantastic people in my life. Finally, I'd like to thank the countless teachers, professors, and fellow writers who constantly inspire me.

Denise K. James

Table of Contents

Prologue xi

Chapter 1 Letting Go of Negativity and Embracing Positive Change 1

Chapter 2 Getting in Touch with Yourself as a Brand 7

Chapter 3 Packaging the Product—YOU! 13

Chapter 4 So, Where Do You Want to Work? 19

Chapter 5 Selling and Pitching 25

Chapter 6 The Art of the Interview 31

Chapter 7 "Flying" that Extra Mile 37

Chapter 8 Vision & Attitude 43

Appendix Workbook

Prologue

I Understand.

People ask me a lot how I ended up as a career coach and motivational speaker. They're often surprised to find out that I know, first-hand, what it's like to lose the job you truly loved. I'm like so many other people—I thought I'd never have to change my career path, that I'd never have to give up doing what I'd always done. I'd had a fulfilling career in radio since the age of nineteen, but all of that came to an abrupt stop about four years ago.

One morning, I was called into the general manager's office at the radio station where I worked. I'll never forget what I saw: people were already packing up my belongings at my desk. They informed me that syndicated programs would replace my show. I was out the door—and they weren't kidding. My show was replaced the very next morning.

What to do next?

The first thing I did, naturally, was look for more radio jobs. I applied all over the country. At one point, I was flown into upstate NY for this incredible opportunity with a Christian syndication outlet—67 different stations were included and the company offered a great salary. I thought I was going to be right back in radio. But it just slipped right through my fingers. It appeared to me that I didn't get the job because of ideological differences. I realized that the whole face of radio was changing without me. I had no choice but to start looking for jobs outside of my field.

As it turned out, I found an opening for a staffing agency on Craigslist. It sounded pretty interesting. It wasn't radio or television, but it still seemed that it could be a decent fit for me. The interviewer challenged me by asking, "Why should I hire you? You have zero experience in staffing." I replied that I had hired, trained, and terminated people for years, I had run entire corporations, and frankly, I could sell ice to an Eskimo.

She had me come in immediately. I was hired.

The staffing agency was actually at Goodwill Industries. Of course, initially I was a complete duck out of water—it wasn't what I'd done for the last thirty years of my life, after all! Not only did I hit the streets from a sales standpoint, but I was also thrust into the other fifty percent of my new role, which was hiring and counseling employees. And then something incredible happened.

I discovered that I *loved* counseling people. I really had the knack for it! And I always shared little tips with the folks I met, even if I wasn't planning to hire them. I would tell them how to improve on their handshakes, their professional wardrobes, everything. I started getting hugs, and real tears, right there in my office. I realized I was touching lives in a major way.

I started doing seminars at Goodwill. I thought it made more sense to coach and inspire fifty people in an hour rather than fifty people in fifty hours. I felt passionate about sharing my techniques and advice. I eventually started to make television appearances—which marked an important change. Somehow, I had edged my way back into the media. Somehow, I had tailored my job at a staffing agency to suit *me*.

The Lesson

Here's the amazing thing. When I started at Goodwill Industries,

I was forced to think outside of my comfort zone. Like so many other people, I faced fear, frustration and intimidation. But I learned that when you welcome a challenge, rather than remaining stagnant, life moves in a positive direction. Think about it: If I had never veered off the usual path, I never would have found my new passion for coaching people and I never would have started my new company, Andy Thomas Productions. So in a way, losing my radio job was a good thing; it opened exciting new doors.

Your own life can, and will, do the same. You just have to believe in it.

Andy Thomas on the air at WARK in Hagerstown, MD

Chapter 1
Letting Go of Negativity and Embracing Positive Change

Here's a secret that no one ever tells you: It's okay to feel negative emotions when you lose your job. It's okay to feel lost, hurt, angry and betrayed. There's no use in trying to stop it—it's going to happen. But you have to know when to step out of the anger and negativity. You can't let it continue on, or you won't move forward.

When I visited Savannah last year for my seminar tour, I met my very first heckler. She was a middle-aged woman who had been out of work for about three years. She came to my program in Savannah desperate for answers, although she was too proud to admit she needed help. Instead, she was rude and disruptive while I was talking. She kept interrupting with remarks and questions. Concerned for the rest of my audience, I finally told the woman that I would speak to her privately after the presentation.

I kept my word. After the seminar was over I made my way carefully through the bustling crowd and approached the woman. She *looked* like a person who had almost lost hope—whose hope was dangling by a thread. Her eyes searched me for answers like a person fumbles for a light switch in a dark room. I could tell that one-on-one reassurance was what this woman desperately needed. She needed to hear that everything would be all right.

But out loud, she was angry. She had covered up this desperate sadness with an armor of pure anger. After being out of work for three solid years, this woman's attitude was full of piss and vinegar.

"I should have a job by now," she barked. "I'm qualified, I know what I'm doing—*where is my work?*"

I understood how she felt. But I also knew that she had probably been searching for jobs only in her field. So I made a suggestion.

"Have you searched in other fields?" I asked her gently. "Yes, it's frustrating to not get a job right away in the field you know best and have always dealt with. But you need to embrace the idea of a *change* in your path. This anger and defiance you're showing the world is the *reason* you aren't getting hired. You have to realize that life doesn't come with the guarantee that you will always have the same purpose."

She looked at me and slowly nodded in understanding. With this gesture of encouragement, I kept talking.

"I was a lot like you. I thought I would get right back into radio after I lost my job. But things had changed, and the market had changed. When I ended up with the job at the staffing agency for Goodwill Industries, I felt skeptical and vulnerable, because it was unfamiliar. But that change brought me to *you* today, to this very spot. That fork in my life's road brought me different opportunities to use my passion in a different way."

By the end of our conversation, the woman was hugging me and thanking me heartily. I could tell that the words had penetrated her armor of anger.

The pain we feel when a job is lost is actually similar to a divorce or even a death. That's why I've written this book, and that's why I coach people during my seminars. I know that it can be tough to let go of the negativity and pain. But once you change that energy into a positive force, you can harness it—and you can use it to achieve a new dream.

If you're a recent college graduate, or about to be one, then you might not know what it's like to lose a job or a career. And yet, the beauty of being ready for change also applies to you. Think about it: you probably have your whole life mapped out, right? You figure you'll finish school with your degree, submit your résumé and contact information, and—*poof!*—you'll be sitting pretty in the job you'd always prepared for.

But the truth is, in this economy, you have to be ready for more than that. You literally have to be *ready for anything*. What I mean is, if you received a degree in public relations and you anticipate getting a job in PR immediately following graduation, then you may be surprised to find that it's not that easy. Instead, you need to tailor your outlook, and your qualifications, so that you're ready to embrace any job that life offers you. Changing your outlook to a broader scope will benefit you, whether you are an older person starting over or a young person starting from scratch.

Let me tell you a story about when I was just starting out. At the time, of course, I had barely begun my career in broadcasting. I was only 21 years old, working in Hagerstown, Maryland. The station was known as "Adult Rock." I absolutely loved it. I played classic rock n' roll all day long, man! I had a manager, Jerry Shell, who taught me a lot. In radio, nobody is what he seems to be on the air—Jerry was really hot-tempered in person, for instance. He was always getting angry and throwing the records around. But like I said, he taught me a great deal about my job. When he finally left the station, I had some big changes to face.

Right away, our new manager came to me and said, "There won't be any more music on this station. From now on, this station will be all talk."

TALK! I thought to myself in disbelief. Oh my God, you've got to be kidding me. How boring. There I was, 21 years old, loving my gig of playing rock records, and this guy tells me I can't do it anymore?

Then he dropped the real bomb. "Instead, you'll have your own radio talk show in the mornings," my manager declared.

I'm not going to lie and say I didn't mope and fret a bit. As the last song that day, I played "When the Music is Over" by the Doors. I hoped that my fans would understand the reference. I had no idea what to expect the next morning.

But the talk show turned out to be the best time of my life. It thoroughly changed me as a person—it greatly contributed to who I am today. Even though I was forced into it—forced to make a change—it worked for me in the end. I got the chance to meet and interview so many fascinating people. Nicholas Sparks, David Clayton Thomas, Jerry Seinfeld, Tom Chapin, and countless other news figures, politicians and entertainers came on the show. And just think, I never would have met them without making that change.

The important thing to remember, when dealing in the business world, is that a seemingly negative change can actually become a positive one. My manager knew that I was capable enough to host a talk show with cleverness and intelligence, that the radio station would benefit, and it ended up being a positive force in my career.

But you can't uncritically accept everyone's opinions. Another boss I had at one point told me that I should quit broadcasting altogether, because I'd never make it. That's the kind of negative opinion that we *don't* need to dwell on—whether it's our own inner voice or someone else's. What if I had taken *his* advice personally? I would have missed out on what was important to me.

Never let criticism or loss destroy your self-confidence on the job. Stuff happens, but it's important to avoid internalizing all the negative input. If you've been dealt a difficult hand like job loss or confusion about your future, it's up to you to change all that.

In broadcasting, (or any job!) whether you are Howard Stern or me, losing a job can, and will, happen at some point. Of course, it's always how you deal with it that matters. One of my favorite jobs ever was working as the morning show host and manager at WVOC in Columbia, SC. The station went through five different bosses, then ended up firing me to "reduce costs." (Disorganized much?)

Understand that I was the one of the top three at the station and I was making them a great deal of money. The fact that they would think of firing me is absurd—but they did, and there was nothing I could do about it.

Or was there?

The second that I exited the radio station, I made a hasty decision. I decided that I was going to get some press and propel myself into my next job. I walked into the office of *The State* and found a writer to pick up my story about being let go from the station. It worked. The very next day Columbia was buzzing about the front-page story and about me, their favorite morning guy, being unfairly cast from the station.

Victory was mine!

The best part was that the reporter had polled people to ask if I should have been fired. Of course, the answer was split down the middle, since not everyone liked my on-air sensibility. Still, it was much-needed press; I was hired in 45 days.

If I had just gone home and moped about what the station did to me, instead of taking matters into my own hands and going to the news, I wouldn't have found a new job that swiftly. I knew what my strengths were and I used them to my advantage.

Whenever you are faced with a change, you have to use your wits and transform it into a positive step forward. Even if you wouldn't quite walk into *The State* newspaper, there are certainly still ways to propel yourself further instead of being complacent following a setback.

The next chapter will deal with unveiling your own special talents and abilities in order to better avoid a career crisis. If you focus on your best attributes, they will help you get through any obstacle you might encounter.

Andy at WKBW in Buffalo, NY, 1986.

Chapter 2
Getting in Touch with Yourself as a Brand

Do you groan when you get out of bed on a weekday morning, dreading the task of working all day? Do you come home in the evening eager to dive headfirst into another activity that you actually enjoy? Too many of us find this scenario familiar; our work lives have nothing to do with our actual passions and inspirations. But it doesn't have to be that way. In this chapter, I'll help you discover the qualities that you could be using in your work environment.

At one seminar an African-American man in his twenties came to me afterwards and said, "I have a confession: I really hate my job. That's why I came to listen to you speak today."

"What would you rather be doing?" I asked.

"I'm not exactly sure. When I go home in the evenings, I have to immediately relax after suffering all day, so I make peanut brittle."

"Peanut brittle?" I repeated with a grin.

"Yes. I love it. I make peanut brittle just about every evening, and I've gotten to be pretty good at it. I have my own recipe that I've tweaked a few times. It's just a hobby of mine I guess."

"Who else knows about it?"

"Just my family, really! Why do you ask?"

"You've stumbled on a secret to success!" I told him. "Think about it—what would happen if you started sharing your exceptional peanut brittle with others? What if you started packaging it with your name and a clever label for your product, and you approached local restaurants and local retailers about carrying your brittle?"

It was like a light bulb went off over the guy's head. "I never thought of it that way!" he exclaimed. "I just assumed that it was an after-hours type of thing, you know?"

A lot of people think the way that this guy thought, but the truth is that your passion can present wonderful new opportunities. You'd be surprised to see what your own personal talents and quirks can lead to—but you have to tell the world about them first. You have to get them out of your house.

Think about it. What do you do when you come home? Do you work in your garden for hours, write stories, or cook gourmet dinners for your family? Ask yourself honestly what inspires and motivates you to be your best. Obviously, the answer is not going to be slouching on the sofa watching television. But the hobbies that keep you smiling and productive are often secret career goldmines. Those passions are what you should pay attention to when you come to a career crossroads.

If you are wondering now how following your dream could possibly make you the amount of money that society, your family, or you have always insisted upon, then hear this: It may not, especially at first. But there is a secret that you should know, that I'll repeat throughout this book. That secret is: *if you do what you truly love, the money comes.*

Yes, you heard me right. If you love what you do and do what you love, then money is a piece of cake. It might not be the six-figure salary that you've thought about (or even had in the past while hating your work), yet it will be a livable income—one that will provide you with gratitude, happiness, and a passion for daily life. Those are the sorts of things we can't put a price tag on.

Let me elaborate on what I mean. At another seminar on the Southeast leg of our tour, a gentleman of about sixty approached me. We talked about how he'd come to a crossroads. He had always worked in the automobile industry, but after losing his job he was stumped on what to do next.

"What makes you happy?" I asked him earnestly. "How do you define yourself?"

"Well… I really love history," he said. "But how could I possibly turn that into a job?"

I told him about my friend Mark, who also loves history, and found his own niche in a particular spin on the history of Charleston, SC. Mark decided to write a book about Charleston's "dark side"—the brothels, the murders, and the seedy stories about the city that the longtime natives quickly forget.

Nowadays, Mark not only has published several books, he also takes people on tours around the area, showing them landmarks and points of interest that illustrate the history chronicled in his books. His tours have become quite successful—and all because he carved out a niche of his own.

"Why don't you become a carriage tour driver?" I asked the man. In Charleston, carriage tour drivers take tourists around the city, explaining the historical significance of different landmarks. "That would be a fun, creative way to teach local history to people. And you may find a certain "side" to local lore that you can really work with, like my friend did."

"It's an interesting idea," mused the man. "I've never really tried to apply my love of history to a job."

Too many people equate work with things like boredom and duty and another day, another dollar earned. But you don't have to settle for that kind of thinking or that kind of life. You can get to the bottom of what your passion is and apply it to the job search. In fact, this task is absolutely essential before you even start to look for a job. If you don't know what truly makes you shine, your potential employer won't know either.

If you could name five things you enjoy so profoundly that you'd do them for free, what would they be? In the back of this book there's a worksheet where you can write them down and really ponder them. Go ahead and start thinking now. Also start thinking about what five things you are truly good at—talents that your employers, friends, or you have noticed.

Note that these two lists—things you enjoy and things at which you excel—are not necessarily the same. For example, you may love to cook, but you may excel at organization. The trick is to find a career where the two intersect in some way.

I was fortunate enough to know, as long as ago as age 12, that I wanted a career in broadcasting. When I was about eight years old, my Uncle David gave me a little transistor radio. At night, when I was supposed to be sleeping, I'd secretly listen to that radio beneath my pillow. I tuned in to all the great radio hosts of Baltimore. Their amazing voices made quite an impression on me. I already knew I had "the gift of gab," so I daydreamed about taking it and turning radio into a career. I sought to merge my enjoyment of radio with my talent at speaking.

My wonderful parents were very supportive of my career choice—after they got used to the idea, that is. At first they were surprised, to say the least. My mother graduated from Vassar and my father has a degree from Princeton.

I'll never forget the day I dropped the "I want to be a radio personality" bomb.

"Mom? Dad? I have something to tell you both," I began over dinner. "Instead of going to college, I want to go to broadcasting school. I want to be in radio."

They exchanged nervous glances.

"Radio? Broadcasting school? What about Princeton?" asked my father.

"Princeton is a great place, but this is my dream," I insisted. "I love radio, and I know I'd be really good at it. I know all about it—I've already done the research."

Eventually they caught on, and both of them really supported me during the process of broadcasting school and getting my first radio job.

Later, as an adult, I made a shocking discovery related to my heritage and to radio. I'd known growing up that I was adopted as a baby, but I sought out my birth parents around age 34. I also met my iconic birth grandfather, Luther Lee Roland, who—surprise, surprise—worked in radio. He had been in broadcasting his entire life in big cities like Washington, DC and New York. Sharing that with him and recognizing the passion we both felt for radio was an incredible moment for me.

This is what each of you deserve: a life of career passion, and of triumphs. First, though, you must know what will spark that career passion for you as an individual. If you've spent years doing a career that leaves you listless and annoyed, take heart. You can rebuild your dream career from square one. The first step is to seriously contemplate what would make you happy.

For recent college grads, the same notion applies to you. If you're to graduate—or just finished—then take a good, long look at your degree. Is it truly what you want, or were you pressured into it somehow by society or family members? Did you get a degree in business when you really wanted to major in studio art? If you got what you wanted from your education, great! If not, don't panic—this is also your chance to build a career.

Here is the big secret: Your education, while it is certainly valuable, is not everything to your future career. Nor is your past résumé everything to your future career. Take what makes you tick and make it work for you, no matter what you did before. Take what inspires and excites you and seek it out in the workforce. Consider this your new jumping off point.

Are you ready to find your dreams?

Chapter 3
Packaging the Product—YOU!

If you have read this far in this book, congratulations! You've given serious thought to what makes you happiest and what allows you to thrive as an individual. This will be the key to the rest of your career path. However, if you still have no idea what really inspires you and what your primary talents are, *don't read any further.* Go back to the second chapter and keep working at it. Don't forget about the workbook pages in the back of the book; they can help you discover your unique qualities.

For this chapter, we need to focus on how to package those wonderful qualities that make you a special product. After all, packaging helps sell a product, right? Think about the last time you purchased a bottle of shampoo or something at the grocery store. There's a good chance that the package enticed you to pick up that product. It's the same way for a human product, believe it or not. Now that you know what makes you a valuable addition to society, you have to package it in an appealing way.

Let's start with the obvious: your appearance. Take a long look in the mirror and ask yourself, honestly, if you look your best. This doesn't mean looking like a celebrity or a model, just that you're representing the best version of yourself. Is your hair cut into an attractive, current style? Or are you wearing an unruly mop on top of your head? Are you dressing in clothes that are clean, pressed, and stylish? Or do you roll out of bed and put on a T-shirt with holes and your oldest blue jeans? Ladies, is your make up professional and not overdone? Gentlemen, is your facial hair neat and trimmed?

These things may seem like no-brainers, but we have to cover them now, in this chapter, well before you even *think* about interviews. Why? Because when you're looking for a job, every time you step out of your house is an interview between you and the world. If you walk your dog and end up chatting with a neighbor and exchanging business cards about a project, do you really want to be wearing slippers shaped like a bunny rabbit and pajama pants? Or do you want everyone who sees you in public to know that you're putting your best foot forward, anticipating the very best for yourself? It's no secret that the way you look affects the way you feel. When you look your best and you're well groomed, you radiate a professional and confident attitude that the world notices.

Throughout this book, you'll see one word over and over again: *confidence.* Without it, you aren't going to make an impression, and you certainly aren't going to get a job. If you already have a decent amount of confidence, that's great! Keep up the good work. But a lot of people who are struggling with their careers have taken a blow to their confidence. Are you one of these people? Do you feel like since you lost your job, or since you've begun looking and haven't made much progress, that you confidence is dwindling? If so, I'd like for you to try this exercise.

Take a moment to close your eyes and think about how you felt at the best job you ever had, on the best day you had there. Remember how happy and excited you felt, remember the respect, acclaim, and praise you received. Think about how it felt to be able to answer questions and serve as a source of knowledge, ideas, and inspiration for those around you.

The feeling of importance you had that day should always be with you during the job hunt. You want to feel confident and assured, without edging over into cockiness. Employers can tell the difference between a person with arrogance and one with a healthy amount of confidence.

The balance between confidence and cockiness is also important for new graduates. You don't want to exude cockiness, since this economic climate means you're competing with people who might have much more experience than you and want the same job. But a healthy dose of confidence goes a long way and shows a potential employer that you're capable and passionate. You should also let the employer know that you're willing to work with the company's standards, since you're fresh out of school. Showcase the fact that you are easy to train—knowledgeable but still eager to learn.

I remember a learning moment of my own quite clearly. At the time, I was interviewing at a Mercedes dealership. I had gotten quite far in the interview process—I was coming in that day for my fifth interview, but this one was with the head of human resources. It was an interesting experience. See, I thought I knew everything about the interview process at that point in my life. But I had an eye-opening moment at the Mercedes office.

Right in the middle of the interview, the interviewer stopped me and suddenly said, "I want to show you what you're doing wrong right now."

Talk about meta-reality! At first I thought, "Is this really happening during the interview? This guy is going to criticize my performance? What the hell?"

He continued, "I think that you're a great candidate for this job. You certainly qualify, and you also give a good interview. But did you realize that you're looking down a lot and avoiding eye contact with me?"

I stared straight into his eyes. "Is this better?" I inquired.

For the rest of the interview, frankly, I was fuming. But I didn't drop his gaze. I went home that evening, still a little angry about what had happened. After having some time to cool off, my rational side kicked in and I knew the man had done me a favor. Eye contact creates a feeling of confidence and sincerity. It was a very humbling moment that taught me an important lesson. The second you start to feel overly cocky, remember my experience. You can always learn something new.

Before starting the process of seeking a job, it's smart to promote your own self-assurance and optimism by having a "feel good" day. Take 24 hours to do things that make you feel great. Walk on the beach, eat something incredibly delicious, call an old friend and laugh about memories, read a poem or essay by an author who inspires you—whatever it takes. The goal is to get into a mindset that's calm and happy. You want to prepare not just your outward appearance but also your psyche for the process. An employer is not going to hire you if you're still any of these things:

- Depressed or insecure
- Angry or negative
- Pitying yourself or your situation

The Feel Good Day helps to deflate those bad feelings and get you ready for what the future has to offer. If you've recently lost a job and you've been stewing in these negative vibes, it's time to get back into the saddle. A day of relaxation can help you do that.

Remember this: Talent does not leave your body. Even though you might feel like you have no emotional energy left after a bad experience on the job, it's simply not true. The same talents and qualities that got you the last jobs you had will get you another one. Even though you feel defeated for a bit, it's good to remember that it's just a *reaction,* not a permanent change to you as a person. You still rock, and it's time to let everyone know it.

There are a few other things you need to get ready as part of this packaging process in addition to your appearance and psyche.

The first thing you need is a **business card.** This card's purpose is to spread your name throughout the appropriate circles. A personalized business card isn't just for salespeople these days; it's a good idea for everyone to have one. The exchange of a card in networking situations helps people remember your name, remember what you offer, and remember to mention you in the future when your area of expertise comes up.

Your card should have your full name, a cell or home phone number (or both), and an email address that you check often. In a later chapter I'll tell you how to best use the cards to your advantage, but for right now, just make sure you have them. Many websites offer a number of cards for free, plus shipping costs.

The second thing to get is a **professional voicemail greeting.** Gone are the days when your voicemail could say something like, "Yo, what up y'all—Mike ain't at the crib right now so holla later." Messages like that convey to employers the impression that you aren't mature enough for the job, or that you don't care about the first impression you make. Instead, record a voicemail greeting in which you speak clearly, say your full name, and politely request a short message, name and number so you can return the call. Also, nix the music! It's too distracting and you never know what people's tastes are.

The third thing is a **professional presence on the Internet.** College students, I'm talking to you. If you use Facebook, Twitter, or any other social networking, make sure that your page is clean—no offensive language, no pictures where you look wasted, and certainly no risqué photos. Employers are checking social networking sites more than ever and you cannot afford to have a picture from a bachelor party sabotage your chances at your dream job. So clean up your internet presence.

You can also use the Internet to your advantage—especially if you're a writer, an artist, or offer another type of service. Create a professional web page to let everyone see your talent. It's much better for an employer to Google you and find your professional online portfolio than to stumble on your Facebook page full of material meant for your peers.

You should constantly think about how you can stand out from the dozens—even hundreds—of other applicants. Packaging yourself as a professional, competent, and ultimately valuable potential employee is an important step to showing the world that you are ready to shine.

Chapter 4
So, Where Do You Want to Work?

Yep, you read that chapter title right. One of the things this book aims to do is empower people—help you realize that happiness can be found and that you deserve your dream job. Start thinking about where you'd most like to spend your professional life. After all, we aren't meant to hate every day that we go to the office, right?

Now that you've packaged yourself into an awesome, employer-can't-live-without-you-product, it's time to figure out where your talents would be a good fit. Before anything can sell—whether it's a candy bar or a car—it needs buyers, right? Think about who the buyer of your qualities might be.

For example, if you're a graphic artist who specializes in logo design, it'd be smart to research new companies who are in need of signage. I once met a woman at a seminar who told me that she knew her calling in life—she wanted to be a product demonstrator. Her next obvious question was "What sort of companies would benefit from my talent?"

This is what I told her: Google as many companies as you can find who would fit your expertise. After that, the goal is to narrow the massive list to just about 10 or 20 selections. This shorter list is the list you're going to research to DEATH. I'm serious. You cannot even FATHOM contacting these folks until you know everything there is to know about the company. Get to work!

At this stage of job seeking the Internet is most useful. You need to scout out as much information online as possible, about everything from the company's mission to what kind of breakfast cereal the CEO eats, if you can find it. Look up all the members of management. Read as much of the professional profiles as possible, and then try to find their personal profiles too. Do they have Facebook pages? Do they have blogs? Make those your nightly reading material.

You might be wondering why you'd need to know about the private lives of your future colleagues and employers. The reason is that it makes wedging your foot into the door a lot easier. For example, when I was running the staffing agency for Goodwill Industries, I once had to meet with the head of a shipyard company because he wanted to hire some welders. It was my job to staff his company and I wanted to make sure he hired our people. So I sleuthed him out—I Googled his name and found out he was from Buffalo, NY, a place I lived for a while. Presto! A personal connection was made.

When I met with him, I had my plan of attack—subtly waxing sentimental about good old Buffalo. So before I even brought up anything about staffing, welding, or any sort of business, I greeted him by saying, "I hear you're from Buffalo! What'll we do about our Bills quarterback?"

He was pleasantly surprised. Next, we started talking about chicken wings, and how I used to eat them at the Anchor Bar, where Buffalo wings pretty much had their birth.

By bringing up Buffalo and some related topics, I established a trust and acquaintanceship with him. Now that he liked me as a person, we could get down to business. And thanks to the rapport I created, he was willing to interview my welders.

This personal connection that helps spur business along is the exact same thing you encounter at car lots, when the salesman asks about your family and your favorite restaurant. Savvy business people know it's the best way to create a trusting relationship. Google those names and get the scoop.

It goes without saying that you aren't just getting the personal information of people while you're online. You're also getting practical information. Let's say you want to work in landscaping. Naturally, you're going to research all the landscaping companies that are within, say, sixty miles of your home. Then, you'll likely narrow those companies down by their vision. If you want to just cut grass and trim hedges, it's likely that any of those companies could fit your search. But if you're looking for a more creative approach to yard design then you need to seek that out.

(I'd also like to point out here that if you are a creative landscaper, or you have a certain view about any career, it's good to point that out on your business card or your Web page. You may, for example, put a photo of your best garden work on the back of your landscaping business card. You'll be letting employers know what you have in mind.)

It's also a great idea to do some sleuthing in person. Yes, it'll be a bit trickier—you really need to put on your detective hat for this task. You don't want anyone to know you're searching for work, so you'll have to be very graceful when you talk to people. It might sound risky, but you'll be amazed at the information you can gather.

It's easy to do the research if you're looking for a job in the retail field. Go to the store, pretend to shop, and talk to the salespeople. But remember: do NOT mention that you're unemployed, searching for work, or anything about your personal motives. You're simply asking what it's like to work at that store.

If you're looking to work at an office environment, visit the receptionist and delicately pump him or her for information. Ask for the company president's name or any other names you need. You can often get email addresses and numbers for direct phone lines from front-desk people. You may also be able to get this information from the company's web site. But scope out whatever you can in person. If it's a restaurant you want to become the chef for, have a meal there and see what you think. If it's a veterinarian's office, bring your cat there and see how happy the animals are. Also make sure all the people seem happy. You definitely want to avoid a place where everyone is miserable, right?

Once you've gathered information about people at the company, try to casually chat with one of the mid-level managers. You don't want to chat with the people who will actually be interviewing you—but rather, people you'll be working alongside with. Ask them about the industry, but don't make it glaringly obvious that you want a job there, because they might feel threatened. You want them to feel important—not insecure.

In my broadcasting career, I certainly never refused a chat with someone who praised my work. I remember people coming to me and saying things like, "Andy, I listen to your show all the time. I'm your biggest fan!" I'd lap it up. Make that flattery angle work for you. Keep a smile on your face the whole time. Never let them see any negativity, especially about your current job situation. Remember what our moms always said: You catch flies with honey, not vinegar.

The next chapter will cover when you actually start pitching these companies that you're just researching at this point. Before the big pitch, you have to get a few things in ship-shape. One is your résumé. Now, there are tons of résumé-writing books out there, so I'm not going to go into great detail about it. I just want to point out a couple of essentials. (Or areas that have vexed people I know personally over the years, me included!)

- Remember that your résumé should never be more than two pages long. An employer just won't read that much, period. If you can fit the entire résumé on just one page, that is the preferable length. But don't make it longer than two.

- Tailor your résumé EACH time you send it out. Your objective should mention that exact company's name, and that you want to be there. Nix the totally generic career objectives. Each employer should feel like they are the end-all, be-all in jobs!

- Presentation is important. If you aren't a great typist, get someone else to type it for you. Use high quality paper. If you're in a creative field, such as graphic design, let your résumé show your artistic sensibility without going overboard.

- If you've worked a lot of places, avoid writing a whole paragraph about each of them. Include the most detail on the most recent three positions you've held. Also, don't panic if you've had a gap in your employment. In this economic climate, no one will be surprised about that. However, you will want to be prepared if someone asks what you did in that time period—such as volunteering, child rearing, etc. Make sure all your information is current—an email you always check, the right physical address if you've moved recently.

- Have a separate sheet of references handy. You don't want to attach the sheet to the main résumé, but if they ask for names, you want to immediately be able to grab them. Make sure the people listed know that you're using them as references.

- Lastly, make sure you've listed a few highlights about yourself in bullet points. What makes you special and indispensable? Your unique qualities in that field should help your résumé shine.

Now, a few words about cover letters. They're not crucial when you apply for a job in person. After all, you'll be verbally stating what the cover letter would say. But if you're sending a résumé through email, you will absolutely need a cover letter. The letter's purpose is to explain to the employer who you are and what you've done—and bridge those things to what you want in the future.

If you desire a position with a (previously-mentioned) creative landscaping firm, for example, but you've only worked at the grass-cutting level, then you will want the cover letter to talk about your personal experiences with your own garden, for example, or in the yards of friends and family. The cover letter can explain how you've tailored your career in ways that the résumé won't explicitly show. You will also want to include Web links for your personal page if you have pictures or samples.

Now you've got all your materials ready—your résumé, your cover letter if you need it, and your research on the companies you want to pitch. Don't forget about simple things like the voicemail greeting we talked about earlier—it should be completely professional before you even start pitching. No music, a friendly message, and a pleasant tone.

Are you ready to pitch?

Chapter 5
Selling and Pitching

You and I have finally come to the most important point in this book—learning all the time-tested secrets for success at finding work, through pitching your talents in an effective way.

Time-tested? You may think to yourself. *If it's an old enough approach to be time-tested, then haven't I already tried it in the past?*

The truth is, this is the same method that your parents and grandparents used to find a job in the days before the Internet. Yet we've forgotten a lot of these great methods because we've gotten so bogged down by the new "applying online" age. It's true that the Internet can be useful, particularly for your research. But when the actual time to pitch arrives, there is no finer way to approach employers than by real eye contact and a human voice.

First of all, I must warn you: You need to be ready to sell. Are you a salesperson? If you've never considered yourself one, now is the time to rethink that position, because you're going to be selling yourself—quite aggressively. People sometimes ask me, "Andy, isn't there another way? I've never been good at sales." But through networking, cold calling and selling your abilities, you will find the job you want by standing out from other, more complacent, job-seekers.

Think about it. Right now, in this shaky economy, most of the world is sending out résumés. But they are doing it electronically. Those electronic résumés, emails, cover letters, and other application materials are often getting lost in the crowds on the information superhighway before they reach the employer. The trick is to do the opposite of that—

to place your application materials right into the employer's hands, if possible. To shake his or her hand and give a dazzling smile. How else are they going to remember you?

Let me tell you an inspiring story about a young woman who did the opposite of what the crowds were doing. I learned about this brilliant woman through her mother, who attended one of my seminars. Her daughter wanted a public relations job and attended a convention with over 1,000 PR applicants. Yet she found the way to stand out.

At the end of the presentation all the attendees rushed up to the front to speak with the people who worked at the PR firms, trying to get a moment with them. Except for this young woman. Instead, she headed for the elevator and waited. That's right—she stood by the elevator until the crowd thinned out and everyone left. Then, when the head of one of the major agencies got on the elevator, the two of them had time to actually talk. The young woman gave her pitch in privacy to the PR executive, who was so impressed with her technique that she handed over a business card and said to "give the agency a call." Within 60 days the young woman had her dream job.

If this sounds like a fairy tale of sheer luck and good fortune, it isn't. It can and will happen to you if you use these personal techniques rather than using the Internet.

Remember that list of 10 companies you researched from the last chapter? You're going to be approaching these companies in person, not electronically, if possible. It really works. Do you need more evidence?

At one of my Atlanta seminars, a guy came to me and told me that he'd actually gotten a job using my technique. There was a car dealership that he wanted to work for, but he wanted to approach the manager when he would have a captive audience. Guess what he did? He arrived at 8:00 one morning before anyone was at the dealership. The general manager was the only person already in the office getting ready for the day. After chatting with the guy for a moment, he was hired that very morning, based solely on his cold-calling skills.

Keep in mind that companies are constantly hiring. If you've tried to call or approach companies and they said they weren't currently hiring, don't believe it! I'll tell you why. Imagine that Howard Stern decided one day to retire from his current Satellite radio show and move down to Texas. Let's say he gets bored about a year later, and wants to do a part time show on the local radio. He approaches the local Clear Channel offices and asks to speak with the manager. Do you think Clear Channel would deny seeing Howard Stern and working something out?

We're not all Howard Stern, but we all have something that an employer is going to want for the company, no matter what. The purpose of cold-calling is to make the employer want to get to know you. People hire people that they like and trust, which is why the personal connection that we discussed in Chapter Four is important. If an employer truly likes you and likes what you present, he or she will work something out with you.

The only way that you'll make an impression so good that your future employer clears the path for you is by perfecting your three-minute pitch. It has to be flawless, right down to your handshake. Why three minutes? Because inevitably, your future employer will tell you that he or she is busy, or about to go to a meeting, or speak with a client, or… you get the idea. So, those three minutes that you are actually with the person are crucial.

How do you make the most of this time? Well first of all, by practicing what you'll say. Make sure you throw in "I know you're busy, and I'll just take a moment." Then they know that you recognize their time crunch. Put your business card (remember those?) into their hands and drop a little "pearl of wisdom," as we like to call it. That could be anything you researched about the company that would be flattering and revealing of your interest. Also tell a snippet about your background, and make sure, of course, that your background snippet happens to match beautifully with the tidbit of company information you gleaned from your research.

The more people that you shake hands with, the better off you are and the better the chance that you will be hired. Anyone you meet at that company—no matter what their job there is—might know the right person to introduce you to. That's one of the reasons that your business card is so important—hand that baby out to everyone.

The idea to remember is to always be ready for an interview. What if you hand your card to someone and they immediately start asking you questions? Instant interview! And if you realize interviews are constantly going on around you, you can try the following trick as well.

Picture yourself in a Starbucks or your favorite café. Imagine that you overhear someone getting interviewed, in a field that you love and want to work in. What can you do? Wait until the interviewee leaves, then go over and hand your business card to the interviewer. Say something like, "I heard that you're in the [blank] industry, and so am I." That way you look passionate, but not like an eavesdropper. Here's another sneaky tip: If you have your phone with you when you overhear what they're talking about, go ahead and look up the company on your phone, so you'll know what to say. Do NOT let them leave without a business card and a handshake—you have to seize these opportunities.

The worst thing you'll ever hear from anyone is "No." I know some of these techniques sound scary and different, but you must keep in mind that you have nothing to lose. No one is going to spit in your eye, step on your feet, tell you your mom is a cow, or punch you in the stomach! There's actually nothing to be afraid of—except for not trying. And isn't this why you bought this book—so you could learn new techniques? This stuff is hardly rocket science, but it's the absolute best way to get noticed.

Once you get your pitch perfected and you have made your mark on the employer, it's time to prepare for the interview process. Are you ready for the next chapter?

Andy Thomas

Chapter 6
The Art of the Interview

In Chapter Five, I spoke about how to perfect your "pitch," which is the approach you use for employers during short, on-the-spot meetings. I also spoke about chance encounters that could possibly turn into interviews. In Chapter Six, I'll discuss how to ace a planned interview. Please note that you will probably want to be prepared for on-the-spot interviews with the same depth. But for the sake of writing this book, we'll spend this portion of it going over some classical interviewing skills.

Your main goal during the job search is to get interviews. Without interviews, you won't get hired, right? It's that simple. The interview can, and might, happen anywhere—which is why you MUST be ready. Imagine that your future employer is so enthused over your three minute pitch that they ask you come straight back to the boardroom or the office. As long as you know how to play it the right way, you'll be golden, whether the interview was scheduled or not.

When I was between jobs, I used the very same technique that I'm telling you about now. I got into my car, armed with my résumés and business cards. I was well dressed and totally pumped up to meet companies and strut my stuff. I walked into a timeshare sales establishment and proved myself to them. How? I asked for people by name, pitched myself, and interviewed with three managers right there on the spot. I ended up being hired.

You have to be totally prepared when you approach future employers—not just with that three-minute introduction—prepared for a full-on interview. You just never know what could happen. These tricks will help you outshine other applicants whether the interview is on the spot or you have a week to rehearse.

First of all, be ready for what I like to call the "typical" interview questions. These inevitably pop up, in some form or other, whenever you get interviewed for a position. The first one that you might hear is **"Tell me about yourself."** Okay, so that's a statement, not a question. But how will you respond?

I always see people mess this up, if you can believe it. It's one of the easiest, best parts of your interview, and yet applicants still flub up their responses. I knew of one CEO who got a forty-five minute response from an applicant. Seriously—the guy told him everything, including his favorite food and shoe size. Don't make the mistake of doing something similar. An interviewer doesn't want to know about your hobbies and personal life. Give a quick, concise answer that includes the research that you found about the company coupled with your own background. It's basically a sales pitch. That's it.

Another question—and one that really makes folks nervous—is **"What are your weaknesses?"** Don't panic at this question—and don't reveal something that could ruin your chances. The truth is, bosses are looking for a response that shows you can solve a problem. For example, when I was applying for jobs and would get this question, I'd pull out my new smart phone and say, "I used to be pretty unorganized. However, I fixed the problem by purchasing a smart phone. Now my calendar, contacts and to-do list are all at my fingertips. It's really helped me out."

See how I turned that scary question into a simple, effective response? It really helps when you can even SHOW them how you've corrected the problem. My co-writer, Denise, told me that she tackled this same question with a similar approach. She explained to an interviewer how she gets hungry during the day and has trouble concentrating if she doesn't eat. She pulled a pack of crackers from her pocket and demonstrated how she solved the problem.

Remember, bosses aren't expecting you to say something like "I lose my temper and I BREAK STUFF!" or whatever your absolute worst flaw is. If you do that, you will not get the job. They're looking for you to problem-solve because they want someone who can solve problems in the workplace.

If you can't think of a way to solve a problem on the spot, you can always use the fall-back answer, which is "I have a tendency to work too hard." It's a pretty standard comeback, but employers are generally satisfied with it—they take it to mean that you'll work hard for them.

Another question you're likely to hear is **"Why should I hire you?"** This is a great time to show off the research you did on the company. You need to emphasize your passion for the company's events, goals, and even challenges. Don't be afraid to share some of your own ideas for things the company is currently doing or facing, positive or negative. Be confident but humble. Never act cocky. Refrain from empty, silly phrases like "Clearly I'm the best candidate ever."

In Chapter Four I talked about making a personal connection with the future employer. One of the reasons the interviewer might want to hire you is because you diplomatically open up—and folks often hire people that they like. It's even possible to make a quick, personal connection on the spot. Are you sitting in an office during the interview? Look for schools attended or sports paraphernalia and make a comment. If you're in a coffee shop or some other public place, watch for what they order to drink, or what car they drive. These clever little observations can help you establish a personal connection—and help you get the job. Don't be afraid to ask plenty of questions and to try to get the employer to open up to you.

My co-writer, Denise, had a situation where she interviewed for a position and then noticed her own sorority letters on the employer's desk.

"Oh, you're a Sigma? I'm also a Sigma—from the Coastal Carolina chapter." Denise said to the interviewer.

They offered Denise the job. By bringing up the personal connection between the two women, she maximized her chances of getting the job.

Another question you may encounter is **"Why did you leave your previous job?"** This may seem like an intimidating question—particularly if things did not end well at your last position. Yet, there are ways to avoid a negative answer. Just don't be negative! It is that simple. Never communicate a bad taste in your mouth about a previous situation—you'll be cast as negative and difficult to get along with on the job. Instead, move yourself quickly into a success story. Talk about positive changes and overcoming challenges. Perhaps say that you left the last company "to experience growth elsewhere," or to "develop your skills."

If, as the interview concludes, you find that you do want the job, it's okay to ask to be hired. Just say something earnest like, "I would really love to start tomorrow." Before you leave, make sure to ask if there is anything else they'd like to know about you, or if there's anything preventing you from being hired right away.

Be prepared—sometimes an employer will you take you up on that invitation and tell you exactly what makes you a less than desirable candidate. If they do this, make sure you correct them and handle those objections. If a reason not to hire you does exist, you'll be able to combat it. But if you simply walk out of the interview without asking about it, there's a 90% chance you won't hear from them again. The lesson here is to handle objections right away.

Now that we've covered the questions you might encounter, let's talk a moment about dress. I shouldn't even have to bring this up, really, but it never hurts to reiterate the fact that you MUST dress your best. Even if you're interviewing at a company where everyone dresses like bums, remember that you're not one of them yet. Ladies, go easy on the makeup and be sure that your outfit is professional. Gentlemen, get a fresh haircut and wear a tie if you've noticed others at the company wearing ties. Even without a tie, wear a jacket.

In addition to dressing professionally, I also suggest rehearsing possible dialogue. Each company will ask different questions, and the ones you've seen here might be phrased differently. Make sure you have your bases covered. Consider how you'll discuss gaps in your employment, if you have them. Be ready to talk about however you spent your time—doing volunteer work, taking classes, raising a family. This will ensure that you don't appear to have been unproductive in the time you weren't employed.

As much as a potential employer is interviewing you, remember that you're also interviewing them. You have to decide whether you really want to work there, right? What did you learn from Chapter Two, when you listed all your abilities? You should have learned that you're a hot commodity, that you aren't desperate for any old job. So when you interview, drop a few hints that you're a catch. Say something like, "I'm speaking with a few other companies—but I'd really like to work here."

Make it look like other people want you, but you want *this* company.

And for Pete's sake, don't say ANYTHING about how if you don't get the job, your kid won't have a fruit roll-up in his lunchbox tomorrow, or your phone bill won't get paid, or anything that sounds like you're in dire straits. You want them to think you're awesome, right?

Because you are!

Andy on set for his interview with the CBS Atlanta affiliate studios, 2010.

Chapter 7
"Flying" that Extra Mile

You've done it. You've given a great interview, you've conquered the objections you faced, and the employer is left with a great impression. Now it's time to really drive it home.

It's a fact that most employers don't hire right on the spot; it's likely that there are other candidates for the job and you'll need to outshine them in order to snag the position. That's where this chapter comes in. Following the tips in this chapter will put you at the front of the pack.

First of all, right when you get out of your interview stop at the nearest drugstore or grocery store. No, you're not stopping for a 6-pack of beer. Pick up a thank-you card. (If you happen to have nice thank-you stationary at home, that works too. But I'm a man, and men don't usually have stationary lying around.) The point is to get the card and hand write a heartfelt note to your employer. After they have an interview, most people don't even bother with a simple email to say thanks to the potential employer. It will make you look perceptive and thoughtful to hand write a note and send a real card in the real mail.

Use the card as a final opportunity to sell yourself. If you shared a connection with the employer, (e.g., "Go Buffalo Bills!") reference it in the card to give it a bit of casual humor. Make sure that you address your passion for the position. Be concise in your note, but mention that you'd be proud to take the job. You might also say that you'll follow up in a few days.

After a few days, it's time to—you guessed it—call them for a follow-up. Ask them for the sale. In other words, tell them without mincing words that you'd love to get started. Ask about the hiring process, and be up front but tactful about it. You want to know if there's anything else you can do in order to get hired. You also want to know if you're no longer in the running for the job.

One of three things is going to happen: You'll be offered the job, you'll be rejected, OR you'll find out that you're in a select group of semi-finalists. If you're up against a couple of other people, then you know what to do—beat them out of the competition using your cleverness.

If you're a finalist, you can do something to make yourself stand out like crazy. And when I say "like crazy," I mean it. Do something elaborate. Let me tell a story about a guy who definitely pulled out the stops.

After contacting a company several times, this particular guy used his knowledge about the employer to grab the boss's attention. He knew the interviewer came from Maryland, so he went to an authentic seafood restaurant that sold Maryland crab cakes. He ordered several crab cakes to go, brought them to the office, and handed them to the receptionist with a personalized note. He was later called and hired.

At first glance, this might seem a little like bribery. But it's actually what our grandparents did to get jobs. It is simply showing some appreciation, consideration and insight in order to make a positive impression. And it works. Remember what we've been saying? *People tend to hire folks that they like.*

As outlandish as your "extra step" might be, it also might be the step that gets employers to say, "Wow, Jane Doe would be great with our company—she doesn't mess around!" That exact thing happened to me, years ago, when I first left the freezing north to take the most important job of my radio career in the beautiful South.

I could tell that the station had really warmed up to me. I'd sent a demo tape that mirrored what they wanted in a broadcasting professional. I thought I had nailed what they were looking for.

"We really like what we're hearing, and we'd love to interview you in person," they told me. "But you're in Buffalo. We would offer to fly you down, but we can't really risk that expense."

I decided to negotiate a little. We came to an agreement.

"We will pay for your plane ticket if you are hired. If not, then the price of the ticket falls back on you."

A lot of people in my situation would have said "No, thanks." But I took them up on it. I knew I was taking a chance, but I was so confident in my skills and ability to succeed that it was worth it to me. Plus, a trip to a warmer climate alone would be worth it. I went and ended up getting the job. And of course, my life was forever changed since that was the highlight of my broadcasting years. What if I had never hopped on that plane? Sometimes the gambles in life are what get us our dream job. Sometimes you have to be adventurous.

That said, you shouldn't pack all your eggs into one basket. Even if you're certain that you're going to get a job—you've even consulted psychics—*until you actually get it, don't count on it.* That means to continue to seek out opportunities with other companies. Continue filling out applications and making sure that you have plenty going on. Having other options only increases your value.

For instance, if you contact an employer post-interview and receive a response to the tune of, "We're still thinking about you," then you aren't where you want to be in that process. In other words, you aren't winning. But you can say something like, "I'm speaking with a couple of other companies, although this is my first choice." That way, they feel special—but they know that you're desirable, too. Even if they say something like, "Go ahead and take the other offer," at least you'll know. However, if you don't actually have anything else brewing in the kettle, you'll feel lousy. Make sure you do.

But what happens if you actually have more than one job land in your lap? How do you decide between the offers? Let me just say that money should *not* be your primary factor when making the decision. You should pick the position that feels right for you. Remember when I talked about passions and talents, earlier in this book? That's what you should consider. Does the job suit your personal skills and goals? Obviously, money will weigh in, especially if you've been struggling financially. But keep in mind that a better salary is never worth despising what you do. Think about it: clock-watching, boredom, or negativity in the workplace are all things you want to avoid. My co-author, Denise, likes to say "You can eat a grilled cheese happily, or you can eat a filet miserably."

This is why it's so important to interview the employer as you are being interviewed. You need a good idea of what that person would be like as a supervisor, and what the work environment is like in case you are offered the job.

If you happen to get offers from more than one place, don't be afraid to call the employers and ask questions to help make your decision. Listen to your gut. I'm also a big advocate of taking another day at the beach—like you did earlier in the book—and letting the peacefulness clear your head and help you decide.

Keep in mind, though, that if you're considering a job in a field that's brand new to you, you might feel apprehensive. That's okay, but don't let that fear of the unknown deter you from a potentially great fit.

When I took the position at the staffing agency for Goodwill Industries, it was very different from my background in radio broadcasting. Naturally, I was fairly nervous. It was different from what I was used to, but I ended up making it work for me and my personality. If I hadn't taken the job because of fear, I would've lost out on a great opportunity. A lot of you who are reading this book probably are embarking on new career ventures, so give yourself a chance.

Looking at the big picture, it's also important not to burn bridges with other employers that you turn down. Make a personal phone call to each employer who offers you a job or another interview. Don't just email them. Remember, we're talking about going the extra mile. Call them up and personally thank them, then explain that you've accepted a position elsewhere. I guarantee they'll remember your graciousness. And if things fall through with the job you take, it's nice to still have them in your Rolodex. So never close off your plan B.

Searching for the right career fit is a process, and it can't be taken lightly. An hour on Craigslist each night won't cut it. The search for your career will encompass everything you do: how you greet new acquaintances, how you get dressed in the morning. Make sure that you're prepared at all times to greet an opportunity. When you spot one, it should feel like an old friend—someone you've been waiting for.

Andy Thomas

Chapter 8
Vision & Attitude

When I start visualizing things in life, it's amazing to me how they start to happen. Here's a small example. I happen to be into vintage audio gear. If I imagine a certain brand that I'd really like to find, at a pawn shop or wherever, often I'll suddenly come across it. It always blows me away. It's like the power of my mind makes me get what I want.

Remember how I *saw* myself, at the age of about 12, being on the radio someday? And sure enough, it happened. I mentally planned to be on the radio and on television, and later in life it happened. Of course, nothing will just appear out of thin air; you have to pursue it.

That's what I want each of you to do. Dream a little bit and figure out what you envision for your life. One of my visions was actually to write a book—and look! Now you're holding it in your hands and reading it.

This is the secret that most successful people will tell you: You reap what you sow in the business world. Put positive energy into the universe; tell the world that you want to succeed. Keep in mind, of course, what we've been saying throughout this book. Success isn't just about money; it's about happiness and peace with oneself.

When I was doing a seminar not too long ago, I shared what I believe about the power of positive visions. A woman in the back raised her hand and said, "I'm a teacher. I feel like I'm slaving away, and I'm just waiting for the money to come. But it hasn't."

I responded to her, "You already enjoy your profession, and make adequate income, correct?"

She nodded slowly.

"But what makes you truly unique?" I continued. "What do you do, in your professional field, that makes you stands out?"

She told me that she teaches a course to high school students on how to handle their finances. Genius! I wish I'd had that course as a teenager.

"Have you told anyone about the work you do with the course?" I asked. "Have you told the district? Have you written a book about the importance of teaching kids about money?"

She said she hadn't.

"There's your answer. You just need to toot your own horn a little," I said with a smile. "Let everyone know what you're good at!"

Remember the peanut brittle guy from the beginning of this book? He already had a gift and a way to manifest that gift. He just needed to share it with the world at large.

But the important thing to think about is this: You have to cross the line. You can't just sit there and daydream about what you truly love without letting the world know about your gifts; you have to take action.

Now that you've almost read this book from cover to cover, the time has come for you to take action in your own life. This may or may not be new to you, but the biggest obstacle between you and career success is yourself. You hold yourself back. But hopefully, by reading this book, you've rediscovered your own value. You now also have a plan of attack.

As the president of a broadcasting institute in Maryland said to me,

"If it is to be, it's up to me." Truer words were never spoken. Take a deep breath, consider your options, and do it! I know that you have fear and concern, but the more you get used to the process of approaching and interviewing with people, the easier it gets. If you're like the many others I've counseled, you'll go through a personal evolution.

While you're going through this important process of establishing your career, you'll want to surround yourself with positive, supportive people. Take note—these people might not be who you suspect. Often, our closest friends and family members hesitate to encourage us to take important risks in our lives. But the people who make it in life—who truly succeed—are the people who take real risks.

Say to yourself the following:

"I *can* cross the line. I *can* do these techniques. I *can* do it today."

What else are you waiting for? Every day that you procrastinate is another day you've wasted by not moving forward.

I'd like to leave you with this inspiring story that actually happened to one of my own staff members. She started a simple Facebook group, for capturing examples of poor grammar on signage in American culture. Within a couple years, the group grew to half a million members who all had submitted their pictures and quips. She published a book based on the group, both titled *I Judge You When You Use Poor Grammar,* and that book has sold about 30,000 copies to date. Who would have thought, right?

Don't go through your life wondering "what if?" and fostering other regrets. There will never be a better time to embrace your dreams, my friends. You have the tools. It's time to begin your journey.

Appendix
Workbook

Chapter 1

Write down what you can take away from former positions and experiences. How will those experiences shape your future? Remember not to reflect on anything negative.

_____
_____
_____
_____
_____
_____
_____
_____
_____
_____
_____
_____
_____
_____
_____
_____
_____
_____
_____
_____
_____
_____
_____
_____

Chapter 2

Make a list of your interests and a list of your skills. Remember, the interests are things you do FOR NO MONEY. The skills are things that you've come to excel at doing.

_____

_____

_____

_____

_____

_____

_____

_____

_____

_____

_____

_____

_____

_____

_____

_____

_____

_____

_____

Chapter 3

Using the example below, think about how your true passion can turn into a fulfilling career for you. Also think about how you would package your product—labels, logos, web sites, et cetera.

Example: Making Cookies at Night -- Pastry Chef

_____

_____

_____

_____

_____

_____

_____

_____

_____

_____

_____

_____

_____

_____

_____

_____

_____

_____

_____

Chapter 4

List the companies that you are planning to contact. List their basic information, as well as interesting tidbits that might get your foot in the door. Example: You see from the boss' blog that he/she loves the book *Of Mice & Men*, which also happens to be your favorite novel.

_____

_____

_____

_____

_____

_____

_____

_____

_____

_____

_____

_____

_____

_____

_____

_____

_____

_____

_____

_____

Chapter 5

List the things you'll say during your 3-minute pitch. What type of feedback are you getting when you pitch?

Chapter 6

Practice answering the interview questions discussed in the chapter.

Tell me about yourself. _____

_____

_____

_____

_____

_____

What are your weaknesses? _____

_____

_____

_____

Why should I hire you? _____

_____

_____

_____

_____

_____

Why did you leave your previous job? _____

_____

_____

_____

_____

Chapter 7

What unique steps have you taken to make yourself stand out? List them here. Examples might be: thank you cards, small gifts, flexibility with scheduling, etc.

_____

_____

_____

_____

_____

_____

_____

_____

_____

_____

_____

_____

_____

_____

_____

_____

_____

_____

_____

Chapter 8

Make a list of goals for the future. Remember, they could start out very small—the point is to move forward.

_____

_____

_____

_____

_____

_____

_____

_____

_____

_____

_____

_____

_____

_____

_____

_____

_____

_____

_____

_____

_____

ANDY THOMAS is a nationally-touring motivational speaker and career coach. His broadcast and entertainment career spanned 30 years, including work for public radio and television in Buffalo, NY and Columbia, SC as well hosting shows on more than 14 stations. Andy's popular syndicated radio talk show aired in South Carolina as well parts of North Carolina and Georgia for 10 years. Prior to finding success with his motivational career seminars, his position as sales manager and recruiter at Goodwill Industries of Lower SC provided the opportunity to develop and test his innovative strategies for helping job seekers find career fulfillment.

DENISE K. JAMES is a freelance writer and editor living in Charleston, SC. She holds a B.A. in English from Coastal Carolina University and an M.A. in English from the College of Charleston. Denise's work appears in many Lowcountry publications and websites, such as the *Post & Courier, Charleston Style & Design,* MichaelMitchellCharleston.com and CharlestonResource.com. In her spare time she's an active member of the literary community, serving on the board of the Poetry Society of South Carolina. Read her work at WordsByDeniseK.wordpress.com.

Made in the USA
San Bernardino, CA
15 October 2016